INSIDE THE NFL

CINCINNATI BENGALS

BY WILLIAM MEIER

SportsZone

An Imprint of Abdo Publishing
abdobooks.com

abdobooks.com

Published by Abdo Publishing, a division of ABDO, PO Box 398166, Minneapolis, Minnesota 55439.

Printed in the United States of America, North Mankato, Minnesota
042019
092019

THIS BOOK CONTAINS RECYCLED MATERIALS

Cover Photo: Gary Landers/AP Images
Interior Photos: AP Images, 5, 7, 11, 17; Al Messerschmidt/AP Images, 9, 43; GS/AP Images, 13; Al Behrman/AP Images, 19, 28, 31, 33, 37; Maribeth Joeright/AP Images, 21; Kathy Willens/AP Images, 22; David Stluka/AP Images, 25, 27; G. Newman Lowrance/AP Images, 35; Joe Mahoney/AP Images, 38; Logan Bowles/AP Images, 41

Editor: Patrick Donnelly
Series Designer: Craig Hinton

Library of Congress Control Number: 2018965784

Publisher's Cataloging-in-Publication Data

Names: Meier, William, author.
Title: Cincinnati Bengals / by William Meier
Description: Minneapolis, Minnesota: Abdo Publishing, 2020 | Series: Inside the NFL | Includes online resources and index.
Identifiers: ISBN 9781532118425 (lib. bdg.) | ISBN 9781532172601 (ebook)
Subjects: LCSH: Cincinnati Bengals (Football team)--Juvenile literature. | National Football League--Juvenile literature. | Football teams--Juvenile literature. | American football--Juvenile literature.
Classification: DDC 796.33264--dc23

TABLE OF CONTENTS

CHAPTER 1

ARCTIC BLAST

It was not just cold in Cincinnati on January 10, 1982. It was the coldest January 10 in the city's history. The thermometer told the story: minus-9 degrees Fahrenheit (minus-23°C). Frigid gales howled through Riverfront Stadium. The wind chill dipped to a numbing minus-59 degrees (minus-51°C).

It was the 1981 American Football Conference (AFC) Championship Game. The freezing visitors from sunny and warm California were the San Diego Chargers. The Bengals had never won a playoff game until a 28–21 victory over the Buffalo Bills the week before. A win on this icy, blustery afternoon would send them to their first Super Bowl.

It was no contest. The Bengals took a 17–7 lead in the first half. They allowed just one touchdown to the Chargers. Few teams had had so much success against San Diego,

Cincinnati quarterback Ken Anderson calls a play in the AFC Championship Game in January 1982.

DÉJÀ VU FOR FORREST GREGG

As the Bengals prepared for the AFC title game, head coach Forrest Gregg shared with them some words of wisdom. He told them that playing in the bitter cold was like going to the dentist: "You know it's going to hurt, but you've got to go anyway."

Gregg knew all about dealing with the cold. He spent his playing career as an offensive lineman with the Green Bay Packers, who often played in freezing conditions. He had played in weather just as fierce during the 1967 NFL Championship Game. It was 13 below zero Fahrenheit (minus-25°C) at Lambeau Field when his Packers defeated the Dallas Cowboys 21–17 in the legendary "Ice Bowl."

The Ice Bowl remains one of the most legendary cold-weather games in the history of the NFL. The wind chill of minus-36 degrees (minus-38°C) in that game, however, was not as low as the minus-59 degrees (minus-51°C) reached in the 1981 AFC Championship Game.

which had averaged 29.9 points per game. That was the most in the National Football League (NFL) that season. Cincinnati's defense intercepted two passes and recovered two fumbles.

Bengals battering-ram running back Pete Johnson—all 250 pounds of him—rushed for 80 yards and a touchdown. Quarterback Ken Anderson threw for two more touchdowns.

The Bengals returned to the locker room with a 27–7 win. They could finally warm up while they celebrated an AFC title. Defensive end Eddie Edwards had a frostbitten left ear.

× Head coach Forrest Gregg is carried off the field after the Bengals advanced to the Super Bowl in January 1982.

Meanwhile, the media began typing up glowing reports. They wrote about how the Bengals dominated the Chargers in what later became known as the "Freezer Bowl."

LEGENDARY LINEMAN

The Bengals had a number of talented players in 1981, but there is one who is regarded as the most accomplished. It was offensive tackle Anthony Munoz. He is still considered one of the finest offensive linemen in history. Munoz was named to the AFC Pro Bowl team every year from 1981 to 1991. He was also selected NFL Offensive Lineman of the Year three times. He was enshrined in the Pro Football Hall of Fame in 1998.

"The fact is the Bengals were just tougher, smarter, and better," offered *Sports Illustrated* writer Ron Fimrite. "Cincinnati's defense frustrated the Chargers every bit as often as the wind and the chill."

Two weeks later, the Bengals played the San Francisco 49ers indoors in Super Bowl XVI in Pontiac, Michigan. There would be no chill to overcome in the domed stadium. But the stingy 49ers defense would be just as difficult to handle—and the Bengals could not do it. Trailing 20–7 late in the third quarter, they drove all the way to San Francisco's 1-yard line. A touchdown would put the Bengals right back in the game. But they were stopped short of the end zone on four straight plays.

The Bengals never truly recovered. Anderson threw a touchdown pass to tight end Dan Ross to cut the deficit to 20–14. But two 49ers field goals put the game out of reach. Ross scored again with 16 seconds left in the game. By that time, though, the Bengals were doomed.

The 49ers stop the Bengals' Pete Johnson (46) at the goal line in the third quarter of Super Bowl XVI. San Francisco won 26–21.

Still, the 26–21 defeat failed to diminish the team's accomplishment. Cincinnati had never even won a playoff game heading into the season. For a team that began play in 1968, it was a long time coming.

CHAPTER 2

BIRTH OF A FRANCHISE

Paul Brown was getting antsy by the mid-1960s. The former standout coach of the Cleveland Browns had been fired by that team after the 1962 season. He wanted to get back into football.

Brown's son, Mike, studied possible pro football expansion cities and recommended Cincinnati. Paul met with Ohio Governor James Rhodes. The governor agreed that the state could make room for two teams. Soon the American Football League (AFL) awarded a franchise to Cincinnati. A merger with the NFL had already been planned and would be complete in 1970.

The new team decided to adopt the nickname of a Cincinnati team that had played in the 1930s—the Bengals.

Paul Brown, the owner and coach of the new Cincinnati Bengals franchise, examines helmet prototypes in 1968.

THEY ONLY LIKED HOME COOKING

One reason the Bengals struggled during their first two-and-a-half years is that they could not win on the road. From their inception in 1968 to the middle of the 1970 season, their record away from Cincinnati was 1–16–1.

Paul Brown was not only the new team's head coach but also its owner.

Expansion teams generally need several years to become respectable. It appeared the Bengals were following the typical path. They won two of their first three games in their first season in 1968. Then they lost 10 of their final 11. They won their first three games in 1969 but just one more during the rest of the season. So when they dropped six of their first seven in 1970, it seemed as if the team was still not ready to be a contender.

Then a strange thing happened. The Bengals started to win. The offense began to pay frequent visits to the end zone. The defense, which had been trampled all season, was stopping foes dead in their tracks. The Bengals won their last seven games, outscoring their opponents by an average of 30–11.

The last victory was a 45–7 rout of the Boston Patriots. That sent the Bengals into the playoffs. But another victory during that stretch might have been nearly as satisfying to Paul Brown.

The Bengals' Paul Robinson (18) scores the go-ahead touchdown in Cincinnati's 14–10 win over Cleveland on November 15, 1970.

On November 15 the Bengals beat the Cleveland Browns 14–10. Brown had been angered by his firing in 1962, so the win over Cleveland provided some revenge.

"For us, that was a very keen rivalry," said Mike Brown, who later took over for his father as team owner. "Nobody said anything, but everybody understood that [Cleveland] game

VERY SPECIAL TEAMS

The first of the Bengals' seven straight victories to end the 1970 regular season featured a strange twist. The defense and special teams scored 37 points in the 43–14 win over the Buffalo Bills. The hero was Lemar Parrish, who scored on a 95-yard kickoff return and an 83-yard return of a blocked field-goal attempt. Defensive end Royce Berry scored on an 8-yard fumble return. Place kicker Horst Muhlmann added 19 points on five field goals and four extra points.

was a little bit like Army-Navy [a college football rivalry]. That's the one that mattered; the others were important, but this one was more important. . . . Throughout my father's time here, especially when he was coach here . . . games [against Cleveland] were meaningful, special games. And we took them very seriously."

They took the playoff game very seriously as well. However, the young Bengals lost to the rugged Baltimore Colts 17–0. Despite that defeat, it was clear that Brown had quickly built a winning team. The Bengals had only one more losing season through 1977 and qualified for the playoffs again in 1973 and 1975.

Brown guided the team to a sparkling 11–3 record in 1975. Still, that season ended with a 31–28 playoff loss at Oakland. The Bengals rallied to score two touchdowns in the fourth quarter. But they fell short of victory.

FROM BUCKEYES TO BENGALS

Sometimes a player's talent does not translate from college football into the NFL. Such was the case with running back Archie Griffin.

Griffin had performed brilliantly with the Ohio State Buckeyes. In fact, he remains the only athlete ever to twice win the Heisman Trophy, the award presented to the top college football player every year.

The Bengals picked Griffin late in the first round of the 1976 NFL Draft. He had been passed over by many scouts who believed he had neither the speed nor the size to thrive as a professional. And they were right. Though he performed well at times, Griffin never rushed for more than 700 yards in a season before retiring in 1982.

"I was proud of my team," Brown said after the game. "They never quit."

Brown retired in 1975, never to return to the sideline. However, he remained the team's owner. By that time, the Bengals had reached the playoffs three times but had lost each time in the first round. The 1981 Super Bowl year would break that string. After that, the Bengals began a period in which they played well at times and poorly at others.

CHAPTER 3

AN INCONSISTENT DECADE

Bengals fans hoped the Super Bowl berth after the 1981 season would lead to a Super Bowl win right around the corner.

Those hopes were quickly dashed. The Bengals qualified again for the playoffs in a 1982 season that featured a long players' strike. Then they settled into mediocrity.

Head coach Forrest Gregg left after leading the team to a 7–9 record in 1983. He was replaced by former Bengals quarterback Sam Wyche. The Bengals did only slightly better the next three years before falling to 4–11 in 1987.

There seemed to be little reason to hope. But just as they did in 1981 after a poor performance in 1980, the Bengals responded in 1988. They won their first six games and easily

Boomer Esiason led the Bengals to the Super Bowl in January 1989.

Bengals

SPEAKING HIGHLY OF RILEY

The Bengals have featured a number of talented defensive backs over the years, including six-time Pro Bowl cornerback Lemar Parrish. But when it came to intercepting the football, the most successful was Ken Riley. Riley, who played with the team from 1969 to 1983, still holds a number of team interception records. He picked off 65 passes during his career, nearly twice as many as any other Bengals player. He also holds the team mark with five interceptions returned for touchdowns.

made the playoffs. After a 21–13 victory over the Seattle Seahawks, they hosted the Buffalo Bills with a Super Bowl berth on the line.

The unlikely hero that season was a rookie running back named Ickey Woods. He captured the imagination of football fans throughout America with the "Ickey Shuffle," a two-step dance he performed after scoring touchdowns.

Woods danced a lot in 1988. He scored 15 touchdowns that season and rushed for 1,066 yards. Woods scored two more touchdowns to help the Bengals defeat the Bills 21–10. He received plenty of help from the defense, which held Buffalo to 45 rushing yards.

The win set up another showdown against San Francisco in the Super Bowl. Wide receiver Cris Collinsworth was one of the Bengals who had participated in the first Super Bowl against

Former Bengals quarterback Sam Wyche coached Cincinnati to the Super Bowl after the 1988 season.

QB TO COACH

Most NFL fans remember Sam Wyche as the Bengals' head coach from 1984 to 1991. Fewer recall that he also served as one of the team's quarterbacks from 1968 to 1970.

Wyche had far more success as a coach than as a player. He lost nearly every game he played as a quarterback with the Bengals. But with Wyche as coach, Cincinnati won 61 games and went 3–2 in the playoffs in eight seasons.

He was not afraid to speak his mind. Wyche angered Cleveland Browns fans in 1989 when he grabbed the public address microphone during a Bengals game in Cincinnati. He screamed at fans who were throwing snowballs onto the field because they were angry at the officials. "You don't live in Cleveland," Wyche yelled at the fans. "You live in Cincinnati!"

Wyche lost his job with the Bengals after the 1991 season. He went on to serve as the Tampa Bay Buccaneers' head coach from 1992 through 1995.

the 49ers. And he made it clear that he wanted a different result this time.

"I've got one of those tiny AFC championship rings," Collinsworth said, "and nobody comes to golf tournaments to peek at those little things. They want to see that big Super Bowl ring, and I want one."

Cincinnati running back Ickey Woods does the "Ickey Shuffle" after scoring a touchdown.

Collinsworth never did get that Super Bowl ring. The Bengals led 13–6 going into the fourth quarter. However, the 49ers scored two touchdowns to beat Cincinnati again. This time the score was 20–16. The game-winner was a pass from Joe Montana to John Taylor with just 34 seconds remaining.

Bengals kicker Jim Breech (3) and wide receiver Cris Collinsworth watch the final seconds tick off the scoreboard in Cincinnati's 20–16 Super Bowl loss to the 49ers.

Montana, who ranks among the greatest quarterbacks in NFL history, drove his team 92 yards in the final three and a half minutes to score the winning touchdown.

Rather than lament the defeat, Collinsworth praised Montana.

"We had them on [their own 8-yard line] with three minutes to go," he said, "and somebody came up to me and said, 'We got 'em now.' I said, 'Have you taken a look at who's quarterbacking the San Francisco 49ers?'

"That's what it comes down to," Collinsworth continued. "Joe Montana is not human. I don't want to call him a god, but he's definitely somewhere in between."

The Bengals would not see the Super Bowl again during that stretch. And in the 1990s, they would hit rock bottom before things got better.

BRILLIANT BOOMER

The best quarterback in Bengals history? Many would argue it is Ken Anderson. But a strong argument could be made for Boomer Esiason. Esiason played for the Bengals from 1984 to 1992 and then again briefly in 1997. He threw for 27,149 yards and 187 touchdowns in that time.

CHAPTER 4

THE LEAN YEARS

The 1990s started out just fine for the Bengals. They won enough games in 1990 to qualify for the playoffs. They even defeated the Houston Oilers 41–14 to reach the second round.

And though they were eliminated the next week in a 20–10 loss to the Los Angeles Raiders, there was reason for optimism. After all, they might have won had All-Pro tackle Anthony Munoz not been sidelined with a shoulder injury.

The good feelings went away in a hurry. And they stayed gone for about 13 years. Owner Paul Brown died just four weeks before the start of the 1991 season. His son Mike took over. The Bengals then began one of the longest stretches of futility in the history of the NFL.

David Klingler throws a pass in 1993. The Bengals had the NFL's worst record in the 1990s. They went 52–108.

NOT OK AT QB

The quarterback position is the most important on any NFL team. One major reason the Bengals struggled in the 1990s was that they could not find a suitable quarterback after Boomer Esiason was traded to the New York Jets in 1993. One quarterback who did enjoy some success during that time was Jeff Blake. Blake started from 1994 to 1997 and again in 1999. His best seasons came in 1995 and 1996, when he completed 57 percent of his passes and threw for 52 touchdowns as the Bengals won 15 of 32 games.

The Bengals went 3–13 in 1991, the worst finish in team history. Wyche was fired and replaced by David Shula, son of legendary Baltimore Colts and Miami Dolphins coach Don Shula.

The Bengals' performance under the younger Shula was terrible. They lost 37 of their first 48 games under him and were equally bad on offense and defense.

The Bengals then showed flashes of respectability. Shula guided the team to a 7–9 record in 1995. After a poor start in 1996, he was replaced by Bruce Coslet. The Bengals won seven of the nine games that Coslet coached in 1996 and six of their last eight in 1997. Talented young players such as running back Corey Dillon and wide receiver Carl Pickens brought hope to Cincinnati's fans.

That hope did not last long. Coslet managed just a 7–28 record after 1997 before quitting early in the 2000 season.

Jeff Blake had strong seasons for the Bengals in 1995 and 1996.

Corey Dillon played for several losing Bengals teams, but he still rushed for 1,000 yards in each of his first six NFL seasons.

OFFENSIVE OFFENSE

The 1993 Bengals, who finished with a record of 3–13, had one of the weakest offenses in the history of the NFL. No Bengal had more than 589 rushing yards or 654 receiving yards that season. It is no wonder that they scored 187 points all season, an average of 11.7 per game. They did not score more than 21 points in any game that year.

No NFL team suffered through a worse decade in the 1990s than the Bengals. Their record of 52–108 in those 10 years was the worst in the NFL. The only other NFL team that won fewer than 60 games during that time was the Arizona Cardinals.

After Coslet's departure, defensive lineman John Copeland said that the players should blame their failures only on the men they saw in the mirror.

"There have to be changes," he said. "Each and every player has to change what they are doing. It starts with the players. If we don't do it, it can't be done by anybody else."

It could not be done by Dick LeBeau, who followed Coslet as coach. The Bengals simply continued to lose, bottoming out with a team-worst 2–14 record in 2002. Mike Brown then hired a promising young coach named Marvin Lewis to take over.

MASTER OF "D"

Dick LeBeau failed to turn the Bengals around when he coached the team from 2000 to 2002. Even so, he made his mark as a Hall of Fame player and one of the most respected assistant coaches in the NFL.

LeBeau was a standout cornerback for the Detroit Lions in the 1960s and early 1970s. He set an NFL record by playing in 171 straight games at that position. He was tied for tenth in NFL history, through the 2018 season, with 62 interceptions. LeBeau was voted into the Pro Football Hall of Fame in 2010.

LeBeau established himself as one of the best defensive coordinators in the NFL with the Pittsburgh Steelers in 1995 and 1996 before returning to that team in 2004. His teams were known for an aggressive, attacking style. Under LeBeau, the Steelers consistently ranked near the top of the league in quarterback sacks and fewest points allowed. He continued coaching in Pittsburgh through 2014, then spent two seasons with the Tennessee Titans before retiring.

"LeBeau . . . had been no worse than Bruce Coslet before him, who had been no worse than Dave Shula before him," wrote Lonnie Wheeler in his book about the Bengals, *The Road Back*.

"It's hard to say when the Bengals actually secured their status as the lowliest professional franchise in American sport. The steady plummet had begun in 1991, coincidentally or not

Quarterback Jon Kitna reacts to a call during a game in 2002. Cincinnati finished 2–14 that season.

the year that Paul Brown passed on. It continued, unabated, and perhaps even deepening, until Mike Brown hired Marvin Lewis in January 2003."

Fortunes were about to improve dramatically for the Bengals.

CHAPTER 5

SEEDS OF SUCCESS

The Bengals did so poorly in 2002 that even playing average football seemed like an unrealistic goal as they prepared for the 2003 season.

But they achieved mediocrity that season—and it was a welcome accomplishment. The Bengals lost their first three games under new coach Marvin Lewis before winning eight of their next 11 to finish 8–8. They even made a run at a playoff spot before losing their final two games.

"Lewis had to construct a whole new culture in Cincinnati, where losing had become . . . seemingly inevitable," author Lonnie Wheeler wrote. "Whatever was changeable, he changed, whether it was players or practice schedules or dinner menus. He was everywhere, talking to everybody,

The Bengals improved greatly under Marvin Lewis, who took over as head coach in 2003.

MOTOROLA

doing everything. . . . In some cities, 8–8 would be an eminently forgettable season. In Cincinnati, it was practically a miracle."

The Bengals continued to improve. This was mostly due to an explosive offense led by young quarterback Carson Palmer, wide receivers Chad Johnson and T. J. Houshmandzadeh, and running back Rudi Johnson. They repeated the 8–8 finish in 2004 and then improved to 11–5 in 2005. It was their first winning record and playoff berth since 1990.

ONE-TWO PUNCH

In 2007 Bengals wide receiver T. J. Houshmandzadeh tied for the NFL lead in catches with 112. Fellow wide receiver Chad Johnson broke the team record with 1,440 receiving yards that season. Both earned spots on the AFC Pro Bowl squad. It is no wonder with two such receivers that quarterback Carson Palmer broke personal records in 2007 with 373 completions and 4,131 passing yards.

Luck, however, was not on their side in the first round of the playoffs against the archrival Pittsburgh Steelers. Palmer injured his knee on his first pass when he was hit by the Steelers' Kimo von Oelhoffen.

"I knew right away that it was bad," Palmer said. "I felt my whole knee pop. . . . It was just a sickening feeling because I knew . . . my season was over."

Steelers defensive lineman Kimo von Oelhoffen stands above injured Bengals quarterback Carson Palmer during the teams' playoff game in January 2006.

The Bengals' season was over as well. They showed enough courage to overcome Palmer's injury and take a 17–7 lead under backup Jon Kitna, but they could not keep the momentum and lost 31–17.

FROM JOHNSON TO OCHOCINCO

Many things have been said and written about Bengals wide receiver Chad Johnson. But he has never been called boring.

In August 2008 Johnson officially changed his last name to Ochocinco, which translates to "8–5" in Spanish. He chose the name because he wore No. 85.

He had already earned a reputation for being one of a kind. One time he sent each Cleveland Browns defensive back a bottle of Pepto-Bismol, a medicine used for upset stomachs. That was his way of warning them that he was going to make them sick trying to cover him.

Ochocinco, however, is best known for his touchdown celebrations. Perhaps his most famous was his "marriage proposal." After scoring a touchdown against Indianapolis in 2005, he knelt in front of a Bengals cheerleader and pretended to ask her to marry him.

Lewis understood at that point that his main task was to construct a strong defense, which had been lacking since the late 1980s. The Bengals took a step back the next three years. They dropped to 4–11–1 in 2008 due in large part to another injury that knocked Palmer out for the season. But the defense, led by talented linebackers Dhani Jones, Keith Rivers, and Rey Maualuga, blossomed in 2009. The result was a 10–6 record and a second playoff berth in five years.

Chad Johnson, who later changed his name to Chad Ochocinco, was one of Cincinnati's young offensive stars in the 2000s.

The success in 2009 did not continue into 2010. Cincinnati struggled and finished the season 4–12. The poor season left Palmer wanting out of Cincinnati. After some pushback from the Bengals, the team eventually moved on from Palmer.

In the 2011 NFL Draft, Cincinnati remade its offense with a pair of high draft picks. In the first round, the Bengals selected

Andy Dalton's arrival in 2011 coincided with a string of playoff berths for the Bengals.

wide receiver A. J. Green from the University of Georgia. With their next pick, they took Texas Christian University quarterback Andy Dalton. The Bengals now had their two offensive leaders for the near future.

The duo found success early on. Cincinnati returned to the playoffs as a wild card in 2011 and 2012. However, the Bengals ended both seasons in Houston losing to the Texans in the first round of the playoffs.

In fact, the Bengals made the playoffs each year from 2011 to 2015. But they lost their first playoff game each of those seasons. The biggest heartbreak came in the 2015 playoffs. Cincinnati was once again hosting Pittsburgh in a wild-card game. The Bengals trailed 15–0 to begin the fourth quarter, but they rallied to take the lead on Green's 25-yard touchdown reception with 1:50 to play.

When the Bengals intercepted a pass on the Steelers' next drive, all they had to do was get one first down to win 16–15. Instead, running back Jeremy Hill fumbled the ball back to the Steelers, giving Pittsburgh one last chance. The Steelers' final drive was greatly aided by 30 yards in penalties, 15 from an unnecessary roughness call and 15 more from an unsportsmanlike conduct penalty for arguing the call.

EASY BEING GREEN

It didn't take long for A. J. Green to show the world how good he could be in Cincinnati. His first NFL reception was a 41-yard touchdown catch against the Cleveland Browns. Both Green and Andy Dalton had a big impact on the Bengals right away. Green averaged 1,173 receiving yards per season and made the Pro Bowl in each of his first seven seasons.

The penalties put the Steelers inside the Bengals 20-yard line. Steelers kicker Chris Boswell followed with a 35-yard field goal to give Pittsburgh an 18–16 win.

The Bengals missed the playoffs the next three years, and after going 6–10 in 2018, the team and Lewis mutually agreed to part ways. He was replaced by 35-year-old Zac Taylor, who most recently had been the quarterbacks coach of the National Football Conference (NFC) champion Los Angeles Rams. With Dalton at quarterback and Green making plays as a wide receiver, Cincinnati fans hoped that Taylor and the Bengals had enough weapons to return to the Super Bowl someday soon.

A. J. Green (18) quickly became one of the NFL's most consistent and productive receivers with Cincinnati.

TIMELINE

1966

Paul Brown and Ohio governor James Rhodes make a presentation to bring an AFL franchise to Cincinnati.

1968

The Bengals defeat the Denver Broncos 24–10 on September 15 for their first victory.

1970

The Bengals defeat the Boston Patriots 45–7 to earn their first playoff berth in franchise history.

1971

The Bengals select quarterback Ken Anderson in the third round of the NFL Draft.

1973

After a 10–4 season gets them a playoff berth, the Bengals lose a first-round game to Miami, 34–16.

1975

The Bengals compile a franchise-best 11–3 record but fall to Oakland 31–28 in the first round of the playoffs.

1976

Paul Brown retires as coach but remains the owner of the Bengals.

1981

The Bengals win 12 regular-season games to clinch home-field advantage for the AFC playoffs.

1982

Cincinnati loses to the San Francisco 49ers 26–21 in the Super Bowl on January 24.

1985

Behind new starting quarterback Boomer Esiason, the Bengals score a team-record 441 points during the season.

1989
On January 22, the 49ers again defeat the Bengals in the Super Bowl, 20–16.

1991
Owner Paul Brown dies on August 5, just four weeks before the regular season. Son Mike Brown takes over as team owner.

2000
The Bengals begin play at the newly constructed Paul Brown Stadium.

2003
New head coach Marvin Lewis begins turning the Bengals around by guiding them to an 8–8 record.

2006
An injury to starting quarterback Carson Palmer plays a big role in a 31–17 first-round playoff loss to Pittsburgh on January 8.

2011
Cincinnati acquires wide receiver A. J. Green and quarterback Andy Dalton in the NFL Draft.

2011
On October 18 the Bengals trade Palmer to the Oakland Raiders for two high draft picks.

2015
The Bengals make their fifth consecutive playoff appearance but fail to win a single playoff game over that stretch.

2018
After 16 seasons in Cincinnati, Lewis and the Bengals agree to part ways.

2019
The Bengals hire 35-year-old Zac Taylor to replace Lewis as head coach.

QUICK STATS

FRANCHISE HISTORY

1968–

SUPER BOWLS

1981 (XVI), 1988 (XXIII)

AFC CHAMPIONSHIP GAMES *(since 1970 AFL-NFL merger)*

1981, 1988

DIVISION CHAMPIONSHIPS *(since 1970 AFL-NFL merger)*

1970, 1973, 1981, 1988, 1990, 2005, 2009, 2013, 2015

KEY COACHES

Paul Brown (1968–75): 55–56–1, 0–3 (playoffs)
Forrest Gregg (1980–83): 32–25, 2–2 (playoffs)
Marvin Lewis (2003–18): 131–122–3, 0–7 (playoffs)
Sam Wyche (1984–91): 61–66, 3–2 (playoffs)

KEY PLAYERS *(position, seasons with team)*

Ken Anderson (QB, 1971–86)
Willie Anderson (OT, 1996–2007)
Geno Atkins (DT, 2010–)
Eddie Brown (WR, 1985–91)
Cris Collinsworth (WR, 1981–88)
Isaac Curtis (WR, 1973–84)
Andy Dalton (QB, 2011–)
Corey Dillon (RB, 1997–2003)
Boomer Esiason (QB, 1984–92, 1997)
A. J. Green (WR, 2011–)
Chad Johnson/Ochocinco (WR, 2001–10)
Anthony Munoz (OT, 1980–92)
Carson Palmer (QB, 2004– 10)
Ken Riley (DB, 1969–83)
Andrew Whitworth (T, 2006–16)
Reggie Williams (LB, 1976–89)

HOME FIELDS

Paul Brown Stadium (2000–)
Riverfront Stadium (1970–99)
Also known as Cinergy Field
Nippert Stadium (1968–69)

*All statistics through 2018 season

QUOTES AND ANECDOTES

The Bengals received a shock and a setback in 1975 when Pro Bowl defensive tackle Mike Reid retired at age 28. Reid quit football to pursue a career in writing country music. He wrote songs for many country stars. Bonnie Raitt's version of Reid's "I Can't Make You Love Me" sold 6 million copies.

In 1997 the Bengals scored at least 30 points in four consecutive games for the first time in their history. They tallied a remarkable 145 points in those games, winning three of them. The only problem was that the offensive onslaught meant little. The Bengals lost seven of their first eight games that season and were well out of contention by that time.

"Go out and play this game like you're a little kid again. This game is what you love to do. There should be nothing pressured about doing your job. It's what you grew up doing and always wanted to do. Just go out and play like you're a little kid again."

—Bengals wide receiver Chad Ochocinco on his philosophy about football

Marvin Lewis was the second-longest tenured head coach in the NFL when he moved on from Cincinnati after the 2018 season. Only New England Patriots coach Bill Belichick had been with his team longer than the 16 seasons Lewis spent in Cincinnati. His 131 career victories tied him for twenty-fourth on the all-time list.

GLOSSARY

archrival
An opponent that brings out great emotion in a team and its players.

berth
A place, spot, or position, such as in the NFL playoffs.

contender
A person or team that has a good chance at winning a championship.

draft
A system that allows teams to acquire new players coming into a league.

enshrine
To install in a place of honor, such as the Pro Football Hall of Fame.

franchise
A sports organization, including the top-level team and all minor league affiliates.

inconsistent
Unable to play at the same level for an extended period of time.

media
The press, or organizations that report the news.

mediocrity
The state of being average.

respectable
Highly regarded.

rookie
A professional athlete in his or her first year of competition.

stingy
In football, a defense that is difficult to score or move the ball against.

MORE INFORMATION

BOOKS

Lajiness, Katie. *Cincinnati Bengals*. Minneapolis, MN: Abdo Publishing, 2017.

Mason, Tyler. *Cincinnati Bengals*. Minneapolis, MN: Abdo Publishing, 2017.

Wilner, Barry. *NFL's Top 10 Rivalries*. Minneapolis, MN: Abdo Publishing, 2018.

ONLINE RESOURCES

Booklinks
NONFICTION NETWORK
FREE! ONLINE NONFICTION RESOURCES

To learn more about the Cincinnati Bengals, visit **abdobooklinks.com** or scan this QR code. These links are routinely monitored and updated to provide the most current information available.

PLACE TO VISIT

Pro Football Hall of Fame
2121 George Halas Dr. NW
Canton, OH 44708
330–456–8207
profootballhof.com

This hall of fame and museum highlights the greatest players and moments in the history of the AFL and NFL. Two of the people affiliated with the Bengals who have been enshrined are Anthony Munoz and Paul Brown.

INDEX

ABOUT THE AUTHOR

William Meier has worked as an author and editor in the publishing industry for more than 25 years. He resides in St. Louis, Missouri, with his wife and their poodle, Macy.